THE Best
IN COUNTRY SHEET MUSIC

Project Manager: Carol Cuellar
Cover Design: Frank Milone & Debbie Lipton

CONTENTS

Angels Among Us. 16

Any Man Of Mine. 10

Blue. 3

Carried Away 20

The Dance 23

Don't Take The Girl 26

Forever's As Far As I'll Go. 30

Go Rest High On That Mountain 33

I Can Love You Like That 36

I Cross My Heart 40

I Do. 44

I Swear 6

I Will Always Love You 48

If Tomorrow Never Comes 53

In This Life. 60

I'm Not Supposed To Love You Anymore 63

The Keeper Of The Stars 56

Lane's Theme. 68

Long As I Live 72

No One Needs To Know 80

Pocket of A Clown 77

The River 84

Thinkin' About You 92

Unanswered Prayers 96

Years From Here. 89

Your Love Amazes Me 100

BLUE

Words and Music by
BILL MACK

Verse 2:
Now that it's over, I realize
Those sweet words you whispered
Were nothing but lies.
(To Chorus:)

I SWEAR

Words and Music by
GARY BAKER and FRANK MYERS

I see the ques - tions in ___ your eyes,
(See additional lyrics)

___ I know what's weigh - ing on ___ your mind, ___ but you can be sure ___

Additional lyrics

2. I'll give you everything I can,
    I'll build your dreams with these two hands,
    And we'll hang some memories on the wall.
    And when there's silver in your hair,
    You won't have to ask if I still care,
    'Cause as time turns the page my love won't age at all.
    (To Chorus)

ANY MAN OF MINE

Words and Music by
SHANIA TWAIN and
ROBERT JOHN "MUTT" LANGE

1. An - y man of mine bet - ter be proud of —— me.
E - ven when I'm ug - ly, he

"This is what a woman wants..."

(Drums & handclaps)

I need a man who knows how the sto - ry goes. _____

He's got - ta be a heart - beat - in', fine _ treat - in', breath - tak - in', earth - quak - in' kind, _____ an - y man _ of

Tag:

Repeat ad lib. and fade

mine. *(1st time only)*
See additional lyrics

Tag:
You gotta shimmy shake, make the earth quake.
Kick, turn, stomp, stomp, then you jump heel to toe, Do Si Do
'Til your boots wanna break, 'til your feet and your back ache
Keep it movin' 'til you just can't take anymore.
Come on, everybody on the floor, a-one two, a-three four.
Hup two, hup if you wanna be a man of mine, that's right.
This is what a woman wants...

ANGELS AMONG US

Words and Music by
BECKY HOBBS and DON GOODMAN

Additional lyrics

When life held troubled times and had me down on my knees,
There's always been someone to come along and comfort me.
A kind word from a stranger, to lend a helping hand,
A phone call from a friend just to say I understand.
Now, ain't it kind of funny, at the dark end of the road,
Someone lights the way with just a single ray of hope.

Angels Among Us - 4 - 4

(To Chorus)

CARRIED AWAY

Words and Music by
STEVE BOGARD and JEFF STEVENS

THE DANCE

Words and Music by
TONY ARATA

The Dance - 3 - 1

DON'T TAKE THE GIRL

Words and Music by
CRAIG MARTIN and LARRY W. JOHNSON

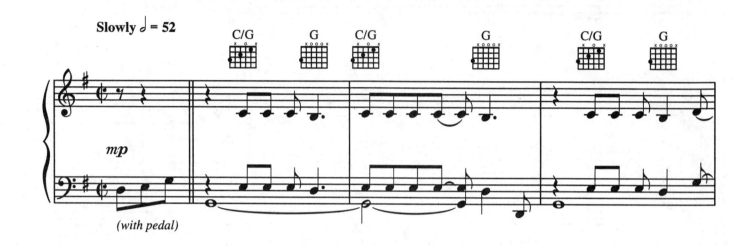

Verse:

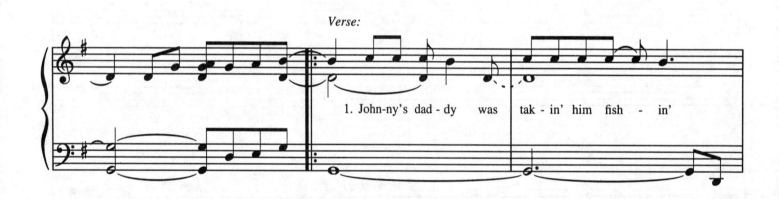

1. John-ny's dad-dy was tak-in' him fish-in'

when he was eight years old.___ A lit-tle girl___ came through___

Don't Take the Girl - 4 - 1

the front gate, hold-in' a fish-in' pole.

Bm7 His dad looked down and smiled, **Cmaj7** said, "We can't leave her be-hind. **Bm7**

Cmaj7 Son, I know you don't want **Am7** her to go, **G/B** but

Cmaj7 some-day you'll change your mind." **D7sus** And John-ny said, **G Am/G** "Take Jim-my John-son, **G**

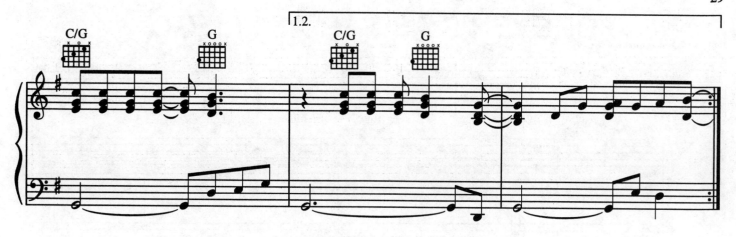

John-ny's dad-dy was tak-in' him fish - in' when he was eight years___ old.

rit.

Verse 2:
Same ol' boy, same sweet girl, ten years down the road.
He held her tight and kissed her lips in front of the picture show.
A stranger came and pulled a gun and grabbed her by the arm.
Said, "If you do what I tell you to, there won't be any harm."
And Johnny said,
"Take my money, take my wallet, take my credit cards.
Here's the watch that my grandpa gave me, here's the keys to my car.
Mr., give it a whirl, but please, don't take the girl."

Verse 3:
Same ol' boy, same sweet girl, five years down the road.
There's gonna be a little one and she says, "It's time to go."
Doctor said, "The baby's fine but, you'll have to leave
'Cause his mama's fadin' fast," and Johnny hit his knees.
And then he prayed,
"Take the very breath you gave me, take the heart from my chest.
I'll gladly take her place if you'll have me.
Make this my last request.
Take me out of this world, God, please, don't take the girl."

FOREVER'S AS FAR AS I'LL GO

Words and Music by
MIKE REID

Slowly ♩ = 69

Forever's As Far As I'll Go - 3 - 1

It's best that you know___ where you stand___ with me.___

cresc. **mf**

I will

Chorus:

give you___ my heart_____ faith - ful___ and true,___ and all the love it can hold___

that's all I can do.___ But I've thought a - bout_____ how long I'll___ love you,

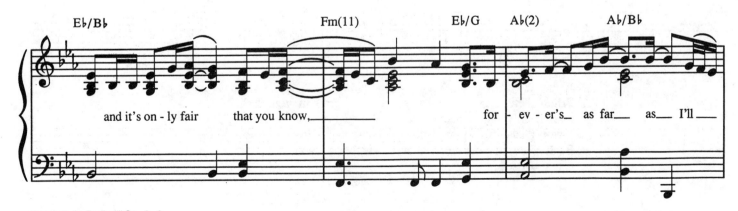

and it's on - ly fair that you know,_____ for - ev - er's___ as far___ as___ I'll___

Verse 2:
When there's age around my eyes and gray in your hair,
And it only takes a touch to recall the love we've shared.
I won't take for granted that you know my love is true.
Each night in your arms, I will whisper to you...
(To Chorus:)

GO REST HIGH ON THAT MOUNTAIN

Words and Music by
VINCE GILL

Go Rest High on That Mountain - 3 - 1

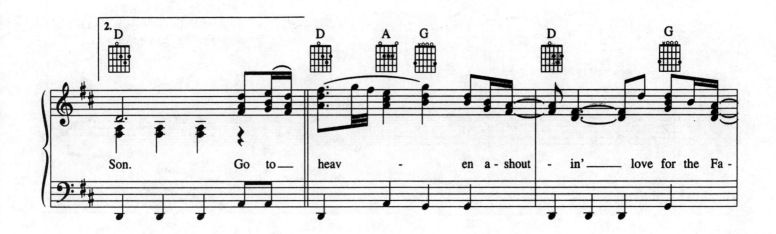

Son.   Go to — heav — en a - shout - in' — love for the Fa -

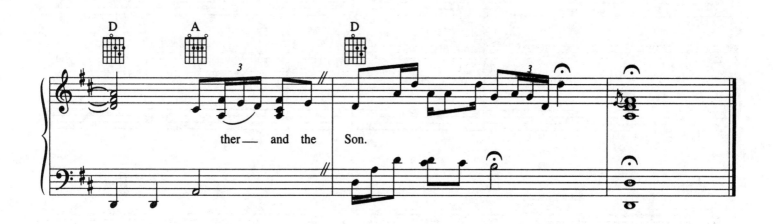

ther — and the   Son.

Additional lyrics

2. Oh, how we cried the day you left us,
   We gathered 'round your grave to grieve.
   I wish I could see the angels' faces
   When they hear your sweet voice sing.
   (To Chorus)

I CAN LOVE YOU LIKE THAT

Words and Music by
STEVE DIAMOND, MARIBETH DERRY
and JENNIFER KIMBALL

I Can Love You Like That - 4 - 1

From the Warner Bros. Film "PURE COUNTRY"

I CROSS MY HEART

Words and Music by
STEVE DORFF and ERIC KAZ

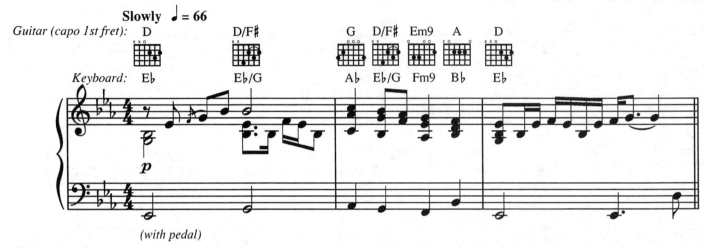

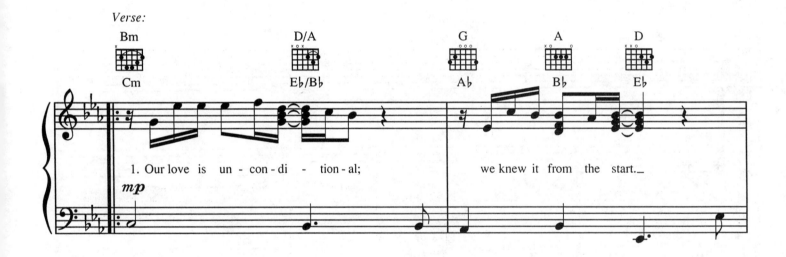

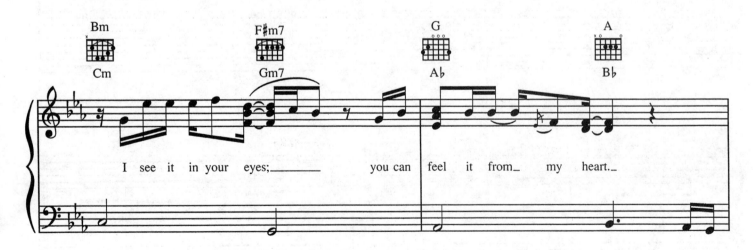

I Cross My Heart - 4 - 1

mine,_

dim.

a love_ as true_____ as

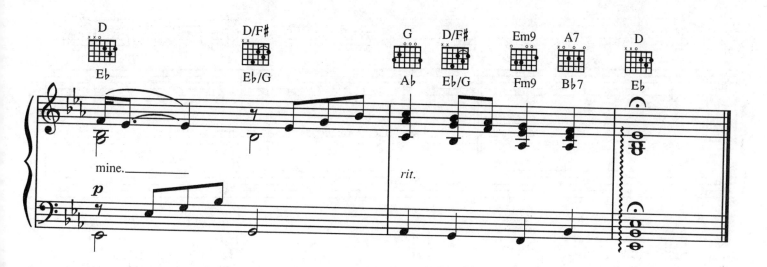

mine._____

rit.

Verse 2:
You will always be the miracle
That makes my life complete;
And as long as there's a breath in me,
I'll make yours just as sweet.
As we look into the future,
It's as far as we can see,
So let's make each tomorrow
Be the best that it can be.
(To Chorus:)

I DO

Words and Music by
PAUL BRANDT

Verse 3:
I know the time will disappear,
But this love we're building on will always be here.
No way that this is sinking sand,
On this solid rock we'll stand forever...
(To Chorus:)

I WILL ALWAYS LOVE YOU

Words and Music by
DOLLY PARTON

I Will Always Love You - 5 - 1

Chorus:

I _____ will al - ways ____ love _____ you. _____ I ____ will ____

____ al - ways love _____ you.

Dolly:
Bit - ter -

Verse 2:

sweet _____ mem-o - ries, that is all ____ I am tak - ing with

me. _____ Good-bye, please ____ don't you cry, 'cause we both

52

IF TOMORROW NEVER COMES

Words and Music by
KENT BLAZY and GARTH BROOKS

If Tomorrow Never Comes - 3 - 1

Verse 2:
'Cause I've lost loved ones in my life.
Who never knew how much I loved them.
Now I live with the regret
That my true feelings for them never were revealed.
So I made a promise to myself
To say each day how much she means to me
And avoid that circumstance
Where there's no second chance to tell her how I feel. ('Cause)
(To Chorus:)

THE KEEPER OF THE STARS

Words and Music by
KAREN STALEY, DANNY MAYO and DICKEY LEE

The Keeper of the Stars - 4 - 1

58

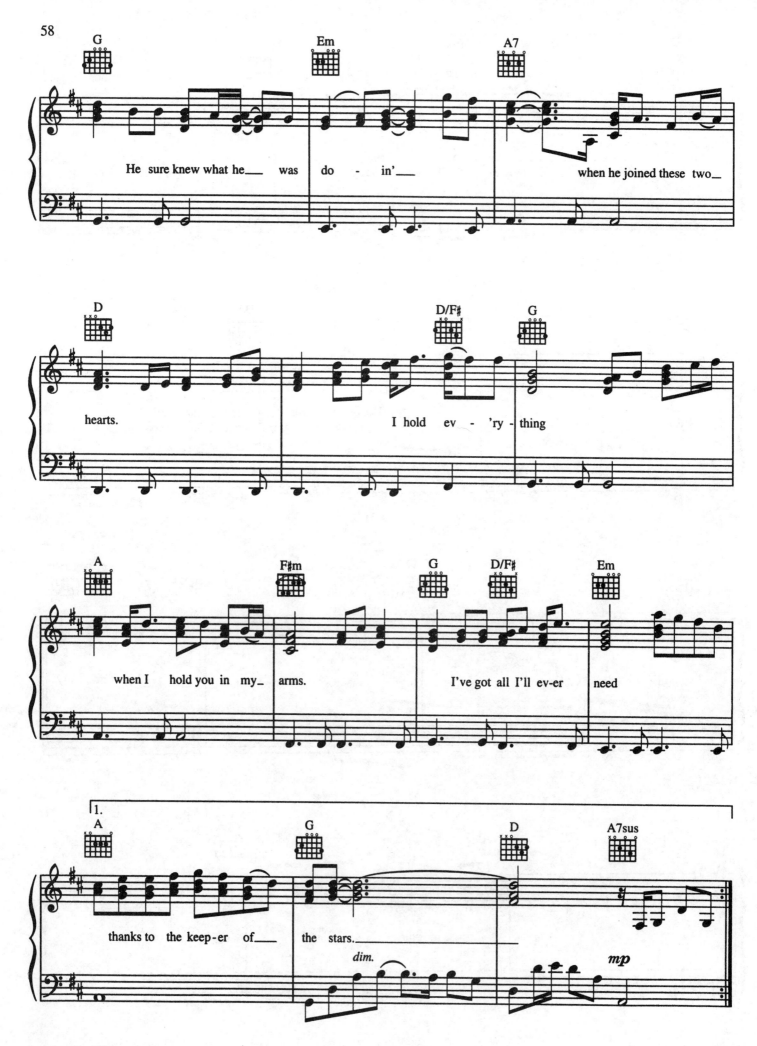

The Keeper of the Stars - 4 - 3

The Keeper of the Stars - 4 - 4

IN THIS LIFE

Words and Music by
MIKE REID and
ALLEN SHAMBLIN

Verse 2:
For every mountain I have climbed.
Every raging river crossed,
You were the treasure that I longed to find.
Without your love I would be lost.
(To Chorus:)

I'M NOT SUPPOSED TO LOVE YOU ANYMORE

Words and Music by
SKIP EWING and DONNY KEES

I'm Not Supposed to Love You Anymore - 5 - 1

64

I'm Not Supposed to Love You Anymore - 5 - 3

From the Original Motion Picture Soundtrack "8 SECONDS"

LANE'S THEME

Composed by
BILL CONTI

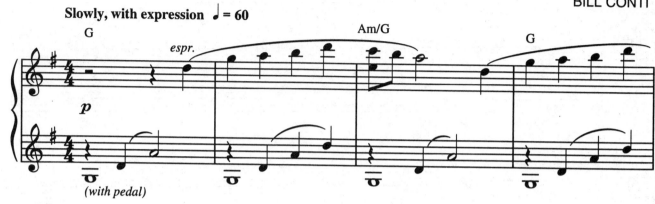

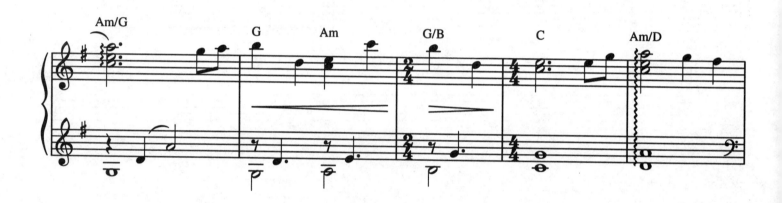

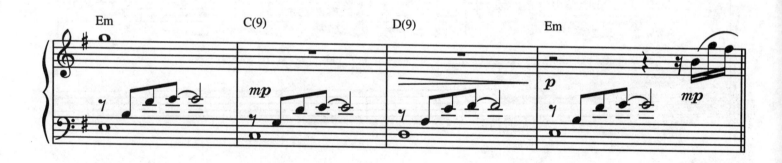

Lane's Theme - 4 - 1

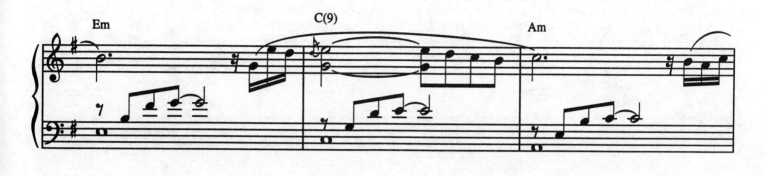

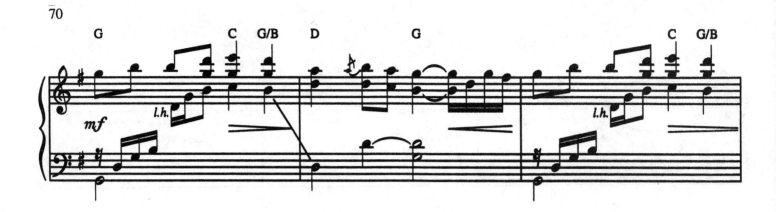

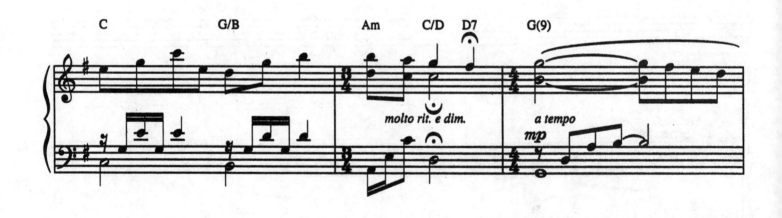

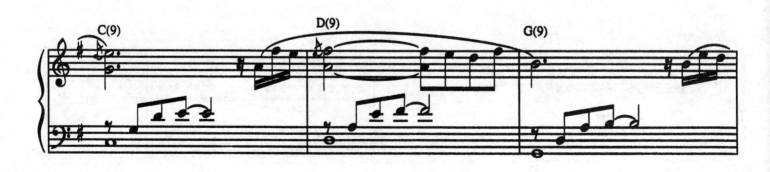

Lane's Theme - 4 - 3

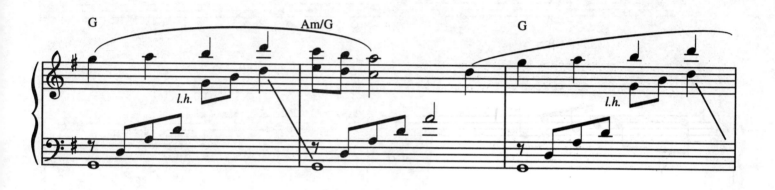

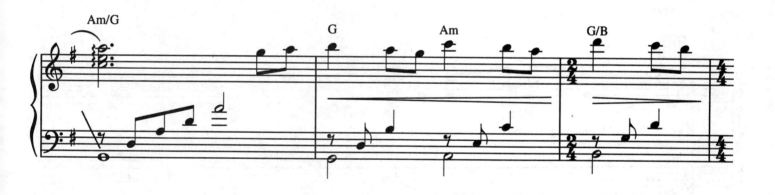

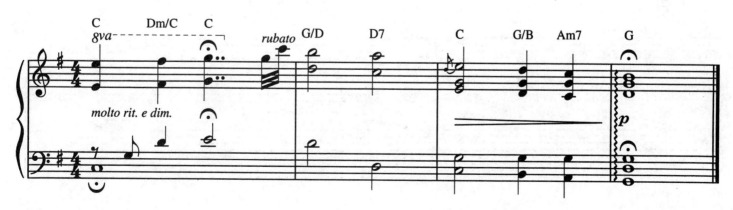

Lane's Theme - 4 - 4

LONG AS I LIVE

Words and Music by
RICK BOWLES and
WILL ROBINSON

Long As I Live - 5 - 1

74

Long As I Live - 5 - 3

Verse 2:
No matter if there are mountains you can't move,
Or harder times than you thought you'd go through,
When the weight of your world's too much to bear,
Just remember I'll always be there.
(To Chorus:)

POCKET OF A CLOWN

Words and Music by
DWIGHT YOAKAM

Pocket of a Clown - 3 - 1

Additional lyrics

2. Inside the heartache of a fool
   You'll learn things they don't teach in school
   And lessons there can be real cruel
   Inside the heartache of a fool

3. Inside a memory from the past
   Lives every love that didn't last
   And sweet dreams can start to fade real fast
   Inside a memory from the past

NO ONE NEEDS TO KNOW

Words and Music by SHANIA TWAIN
and ROBERT JOHN "MUTT" LANGE

* Vocal sung one octave lower.

No One Needs to Know - 4 - 1

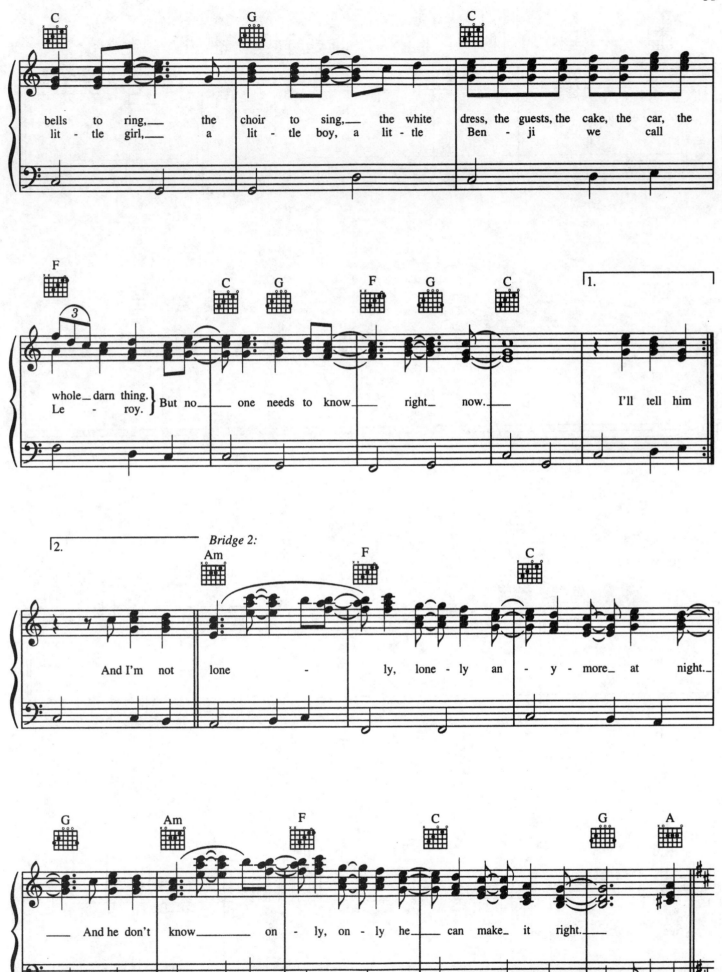

(Instrumental solo...

...end solo) And I'm not

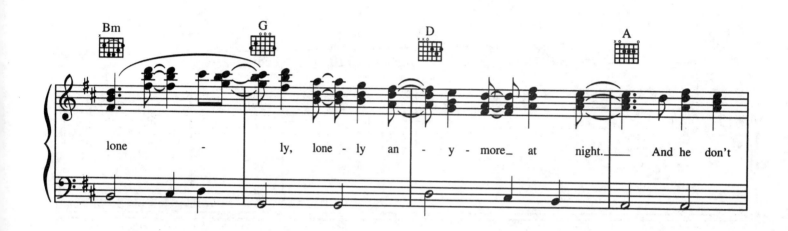

lone - ly, lone-ly an - y-more_ at night._ And he don't

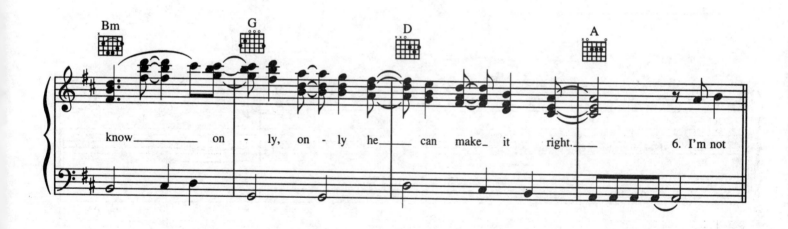

know_____ on - ly, on-ly he_ can make_ it right.___ 6. I'm not

dream-in'___ or stu-pid,_ but boy, have I been hit by Cu - pid.___ But no_

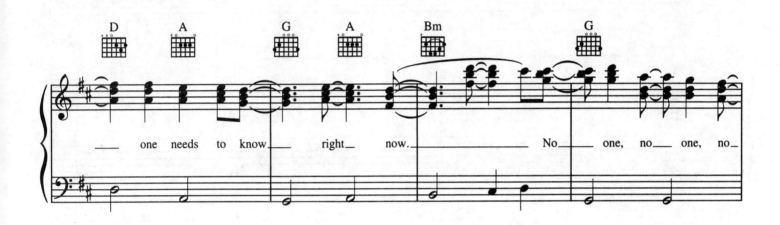

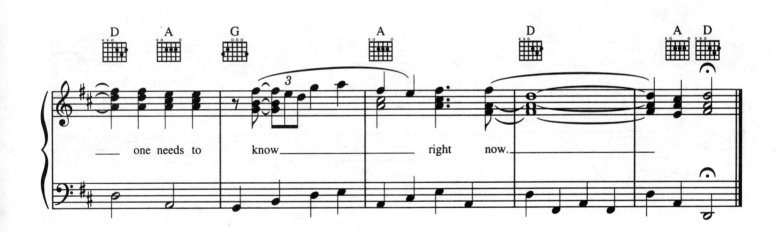

Verse 2:
I met a tall, dark and handsome man.
And I've been busy makin' big plans.
But no one needs to know right now.
(To Verse 3:)

Verse 3:
I got my heart set, my feet wet,
And he don't even know yet.
But no one needs to know right now.
(To Bridge 1:)

THE RIVER

Words and Music by
VICTORIA SHAW and GARTH BROOKS

The River - 5 - 1

86

if I nev-er try. So, I will___ sail my ves-sel 'til the

riv-er runs_ dry. Yes, I will sail my ves-sel 'til the

riv-er runs_ dry. 'til the riv-er runs_ dry.___

(1st time only)

Verse 2:
Too many times we stand aside
And let the waters slip away
'Til what we put off 'til tomorrow
Has now become today.
So, don't you sit upon the shoreline
And say you're satisfied.
Choose to chance the rapids
And dare to dance the tide. Yes, I will . . .
(To Chorus:)

YEARS FROM HERE

Words and Music by
GARY BAKER, JERRY WILLIAMS
and FRANK J. MYERS

1. Stand - ing here face to face,_____ I feel my heart
2. I can prom - ise you this_____ with ev - 'ry breath

___ o - ver - flow - ing with love and e - mo - tion. The mo - ment you took my hand,
___ I take,___ I'll live to love___ you. I'll go a - bove and be - yond

___ there was no doubt___ in my mind___ a - bout our fu - ture.
to give you ev - 'ry - thing___ that one man can give___ you.

Years from Here - 3 - 1

THINKIN' ABOUT YOU

Moderately ♩ = 92

Words and Music by
TOM SHAPIRO and BOB REGAN

Verse 1:

1. I'm not quite sure what's go-in' on, but all day through and all night long, I've been think-in' a-bout you, I've been think-in' a-bout you.

Verse 2:

2. The look in your eyes when you

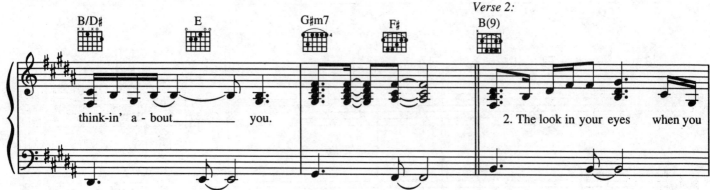

Thinkin' About You - 4 - 1

smile that way,___ the sound of your voice say - in' my name.___ I've been

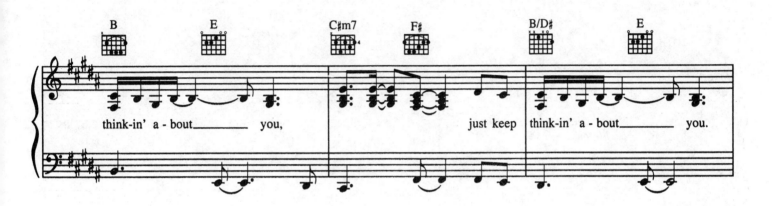

think-in' a - bout___ you, just keep think-in' a - bout___ you.

℅ *Bridge:*

This sin - gle - mind - ed fas - ci - na - tion I've got,___

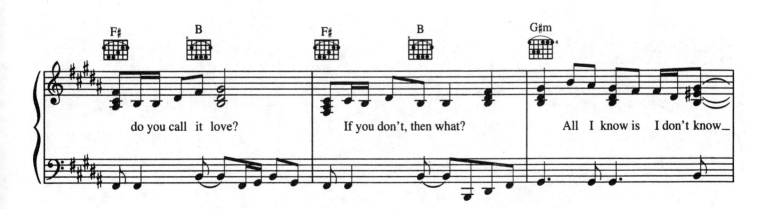

do you call it love? If you don't, then what? All I know is I don't know___

_____ what you've done,_ and this train of thought_ ain't a-bout to jump_ the track that it's on.___

Verses 3 & 4:

3. In the back of my mind, there's a se - cret place._ But the whole world knows by the
4. *See additional lyrics*

smile on my face___ that I've been think-in' a - bout___ you.

To Coda ⊕

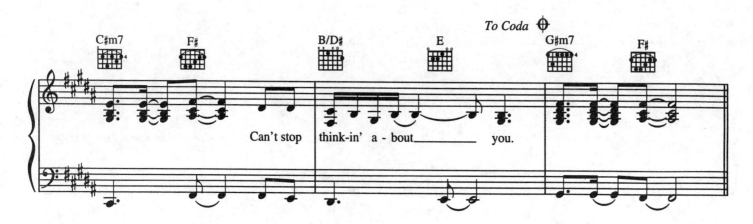

Can't stop think-in' a - bout___ you.

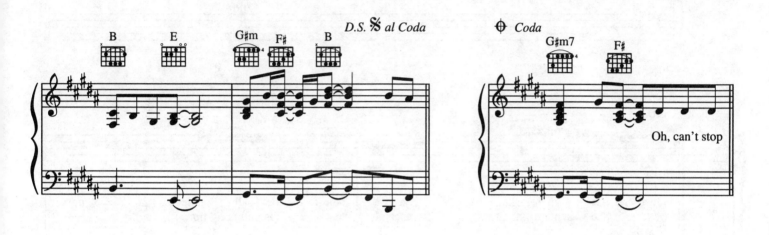

D.S. 𝄋 *al Coda*   ⊕ *Coda*

Oh, can't stop

Repeat ad lib. and fade

think-in' a-bout_ you._   I'm al-ways   think-in' a-bout_ you._   Oh, I do love

Verse 4:
I know it's crazy, callin' you this late,
When the only thing I wanted to say is that
I've been thinkin' about you,
Oh, just keep thinkin' about you.

Thinkin' About You - 4 - 4

UNANSWERED PRAYERS

Words and Music by
LARRY B. BASTIAN, PAT ALGER
and GARTH BROOKS

Slowly ♩ = 66

with pedal

Verse:

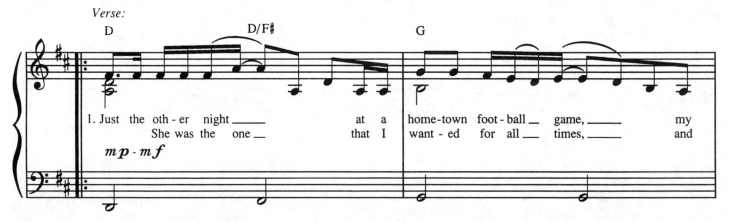

1. Just the oth-er night _____ at a home-town foot-ball _ game, _____ my
   She was the one _ that I want-ed for all _ times, _____ and

wife and I ran in-to _____ my old high school _ flame. And
each night I'd spend pray-ing _ that God would make her _ mine. And

as I in-tro-duced _ them _ the past came back to me _____ and I
if He'd on-ly grant _ me _ this wish I'd wished back then _____ I'd

Unanswered Prayers - 4 - 1

98

looked at my wife, _____ and then and there I thanked the good _ Lord for the

gifts in my life. _____ *cresc.* Some-times I ___ thank

Coda ⊕
are un - an - swered, some of God's great - est gifts are all too

of - ten un - an - swered, some of God's great-est gifts are un - an - swered prayers. _

dim. *mf* *rit.*

YOUR LOVE AMAZES ME

Words and Music by
CHUCK JONES and AMANDA HUNT

Your Love Amazes Me - 4 - 1

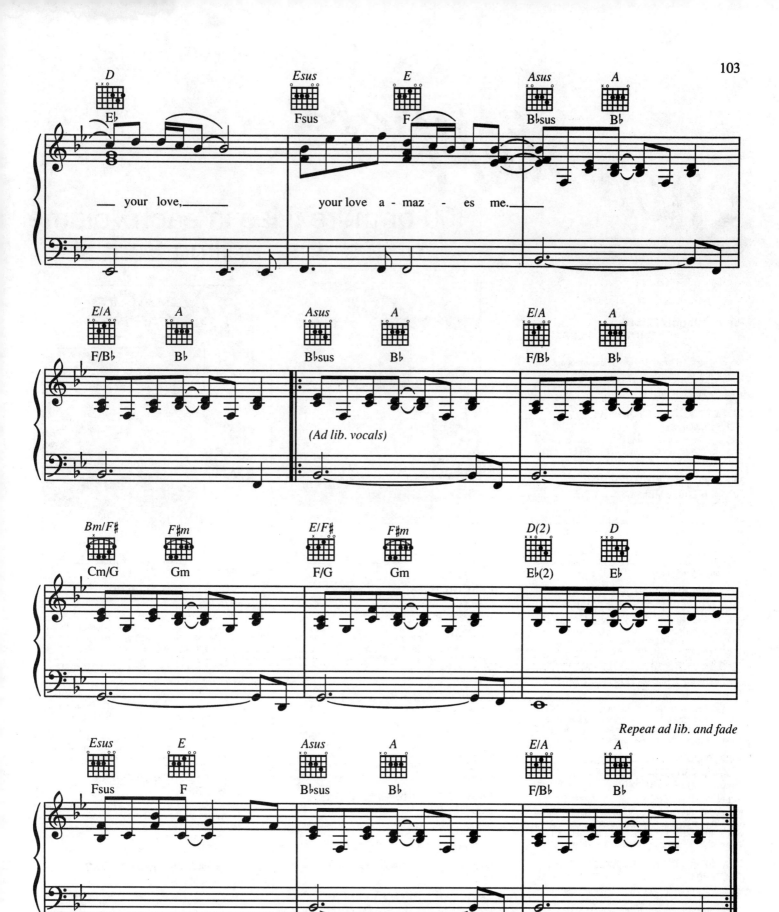

Verse 2:

I've seen a sunset that would make you cry,
And colors of a rainbow reaching 'cross the sky.
The moon in all its phases, but
Your love amazes me.
To Chorus:

Verse 3:

I've prayed for miracles that never came.
I got down on my knees in the pouring rain.
But only you could save me,
Your love amazes me.
(To Chorus:)

Showstoppers

100 or more titles in each volume of this Best-Selling Series!

Piano/Vocal/Chords:
20's, 30's, & 40's SHOWSTOPPERS
(F2865SMX)

100 nostalgic favorites include: Chattanooga Choo Choo ● Pennsylvania 6-5000 ● Blue Moon ● Moonglow ● My Blue Heaven ● Ain't Misbehavin' ● That Old Black Magic and more.

50's & 60's SHOWSTOPPERS
(F2864SMB)

Bop back to a simpler time and enjoy: Aquarius/Let the Sunshine In ● (Sittin' On) The Dock of the Bay ● Hey, Good Lookin' ● Sunny ● Johnny Angel and more.

70's & 80's SHOWSTOPPERS
P/V/C (F2863SME)
Easy Piano (F2863P2X)

100 pop songs from two decades. Titles include: Anything for You ● Blue Bayou ● Hungry Eyes ● I Wanna Dance with Somebody (Who Loves Me) ● If You Say My Eyes Are Beautiful ● I'll Never Love This Way Again ● Isn't She Lovely ● Old Time Rock & Roll ● When the Night Comes.

BIG NOTE PIANO SHOWSTOPPERS
Vol. 1 (F2871P3C)   Vol. 2 (F2918P3A)

Easy-to-read big note arrangements of 100 popular tunes include: Do You Want to Know a Secret? ● If Ever You're in My Arms Again ● Moon River ● Over the Rainbow ● Singin' in the Rain ● You Light Up My Life ● Theme from *Love Story*.

BROADWAY SHOWSTOPPERS
(F2878SMB)

100 great show tunes include: Ain't Misbehavin' ● Almost Like Being in Love ● Consider Yourself ● Give My Regards to Broadway ● Good Morning Starshine ● Mood Indigo ● Send in the Clowns ● Tomorrow.

CHRISTMAS SHOWSTOPPERS
P/V/C (F2868SMA)
Easy Piano (F2924P2X)
Big Note (F2925P3X)

100 favorite holiday songs including: Sleigh Ride ● Silver Bells ● Deck the Halls ● Have Yourself a Merry Little Christmas ● Here Comes Santa Claus ● Little Drummer Boy ● Let It Snow! Let It Snow! Let It Snow!

CLASSICAL PIANO SHOWSTOPPERS
(F2872P9X)

100 classical intermediate piano solos include: Arioso ● Bridal Chorus (from *Lohengrin*) ● Clair de Lune ● Fifth Symphony (Theme) ● Minuet in G ● Moonlight Sonata (1st Movement) ● Polovetsian Dance (from *Prince Igor*) ● The Swan ● Wedding March (from *A Midsummer Night's Dream*).

COUNTRY SHOWSTOPPERS
(F2902SMC)

A fine collection of 101 favorite country classics and standards including: Cold, Cold Heart ● For the Good Times ● I'm So Lonesome I Could Cry ● There's a Tear in My Beer ● Young Country and more.

EASY GUITAR SHOWSTOPPERS
(F2934EGA)

100 guitar arrangements of new chart hits, old favorites, classics and solid gold songs. Includes melody, chords and lyrics for songs like: Didn't We ● Love Theme from *St. Elmo's Fire* (For Just a Moment) ● Out Here on My Own ● Please Mr. Postman ● Proud Mary ● The Way He Makes Me Feel ● With You I'm Born Again ● You're the Inspiration.

EASY LISTENING SHOWSTOPPERS
(F3069SMX)

85 easy listening songs including popular favorites, standards, TV and movie selections like: After All (Love Theme from *Chances Are*) ● From a Distance ● The Greatest Love of All ● Here We Are ● Theme from *Ice Castles* (Through the Eyes of Love) ● The Vows Go Unbroken (Always True to You) ● You Are So Beautiful.

EASY ORGAN SHOWSTOPPERS
(F2873EOB)

100 great current hits and timeless standards in easy arrangements for organ include: After the Lovin' ● Always and Forever ● Come Saturday Morning ● I Just Called to Say I Love You ● Isn't She Lovely ● On the Wings of Love ● Up Where We Belong ● You Light Up My Life.

EASY PIANO SHOWSTOPPERS
Vol. 1 (F2875P2D)   Vol. 2 (F2912P2C)

100 easy piano arrangements of familiar songs include: Alfie ● Baby Elephant Walk ● Classical Gas ● Don't Cry Out Loud ● Colour My World ● The Pink Panther ● I Honestly Love You.

JAZZ SHOWSTOPPERS
(F2953SMX)

101 standard jazz tunes including: Misty ● Elmer's Tune ● Birth of the Blues ● It Don't Mean a Thing (If It Ain't Got That Swing).

MOVIE SHOWSTOPPERS
(F2866SMC)

100 songs from memorable motion pictures include: Axel F ● Up Where We Belong ● Speak Softly Love (from *The Godfather*) ● The Entertainer ● Fame ● Nine to Five ● Nobody Does It Better.

POPULAR PIANO SHOWSTOPPERS
(F2876P9B)

100 popular intermediate piano solos include: Baby Elephant Walk ● Gonna Fly Now (Theme from *Rocky*) ● The Hill Street Blues Theme ● Love Is a Many-Splendored Thing ● (Love Theme from) *Romeo and Juliet* ● Separate Lives (Love Theme from *White Nights*) ● The Shadow of Your Smile ● Theme from *The Apartment* ● Theme from *New York, New York*.

RAGTIME SHOWSTOPPERS
(F2867SMX)

These 100 original classic rags by Scott Joplin, James Scott, Joseph Lamb and other ragtime composers include: Maple Leaf Rag ● The Entertainer ● Kansas City Rag ● Ma Rag Time Baby ● The St. Louis Rag ● World's Fair Rag and many others.

ROMANTIC SHOWSTOPPERS
(F2870SMC)

101 beautiful songs including: After All (Love Theme from *Chances Are*) ● Here and Now ● I Can't Stop Loving You ● If You Say My Eyes Are Beautiful ● The Vows Go Unbroken (Always True to You) ● You Got It.

TELEVISION SHOWSTOPPERS
(F2874SMC)

103 TV themes including: Another World ● Dear John ● Hall or Nothing (The Arsenio Hall Show) ● Star Trek -The Next Generation (Main Title) ● Theme from "Cheers" (Where Everybody Knows Your Name).